Amazing life cycles
MINIBEASTS

by George C. McGavin

ticktock

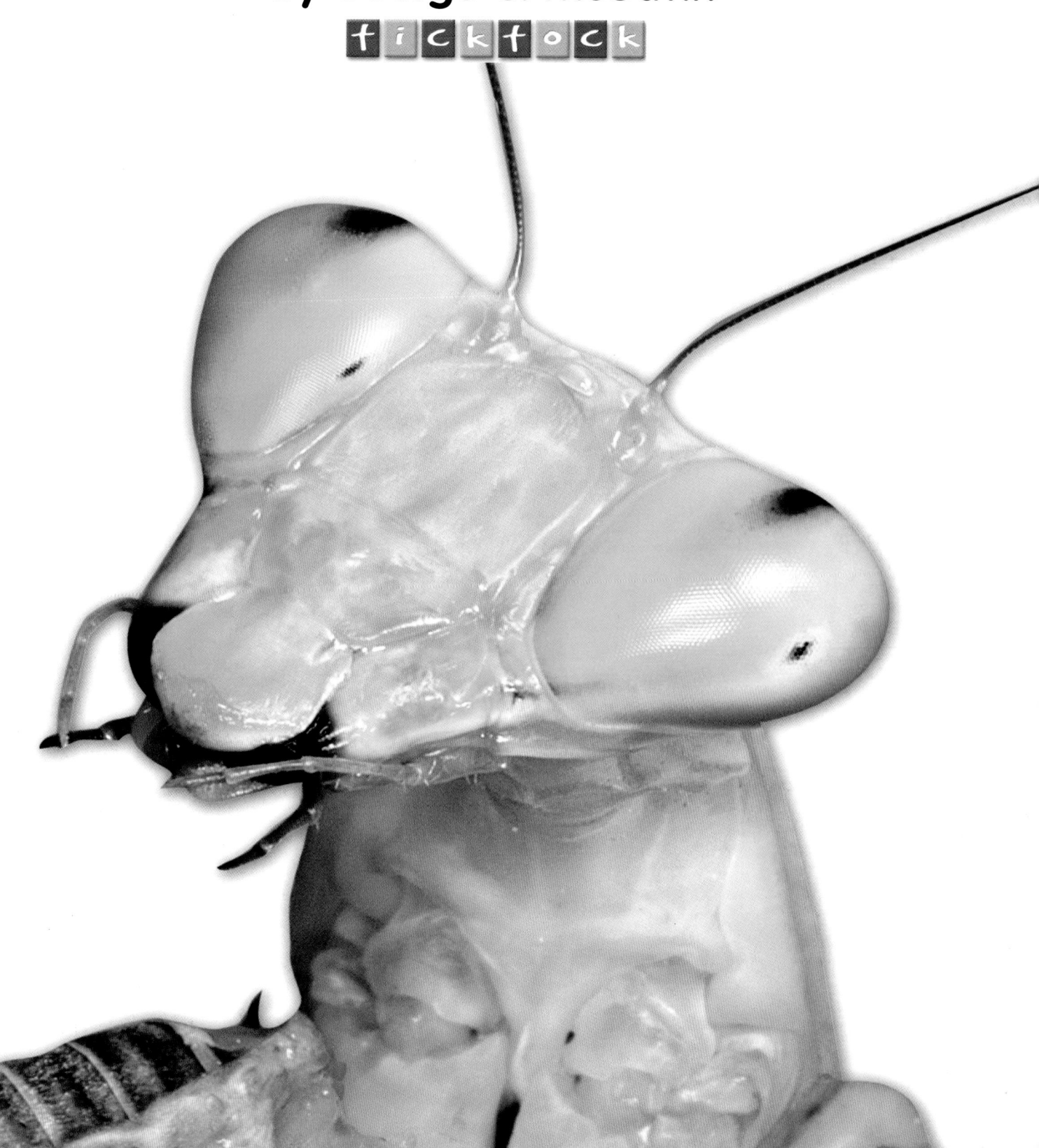

Copyright © ticktock Entertainment Ltd 2007

First published in Great Britain in 2007 by ticktock Media Ltd,
2 Orchard Business Centre, North Farm Road, Tunbridge Wells, Kent, TN2 3XF

ticktock project editor: Ruth Owen
ticktock project designer: Sara Greasley
With thanks to: Trudi Webb, Sally Morgan and Elizabeth Wiggans

ISBN 978-1-84696-073-4 pbk

Printed in China
9 8 7 6 5 4 3

A CIP catalogue record for this book is available from the British Library.

Picture credits (t=top; b=bottom; c=centre; l=left; r=right):
FLPA: 14cl, 16tl, 16 main, 17t, 21tr, 21br, 24, 25, 28 main, 29. Nature Picture Library: 7cl, 7r, 11b, 15cl, 22c, 22b, 27t, 30b.
NHPA: 11t, 27b. Shutterstock: OFC, 1, 2, 3, 4, 5, 6, 7t, 8, 9, 10, 11cr, 12tl, 13, 14tl, 14ct, 14b, 15t, 15cr, 15c, 15bl, 15br, 17b, 18,
19, 20tl, 20–21 main, 22tl, 23, 26, 28tl, 30tl, 31, OBC. ticktock image archive: map page 12, 14cr.

Every effort has been made to trace copyright holders, and we apologise in advance for any omissions. We would be
pleased to insert the appropriate acknowledgments in any subsequent edition of this publication.

Contents

Words that look
bold like this
are in the glossary.

Whut is an insect:

Insects are a group of animals which include bees, butterflies, ants and beetles. All insects have six legs and a body in three parts. The sections of an insect's body are called the head, **thorax** and **abdomen**.

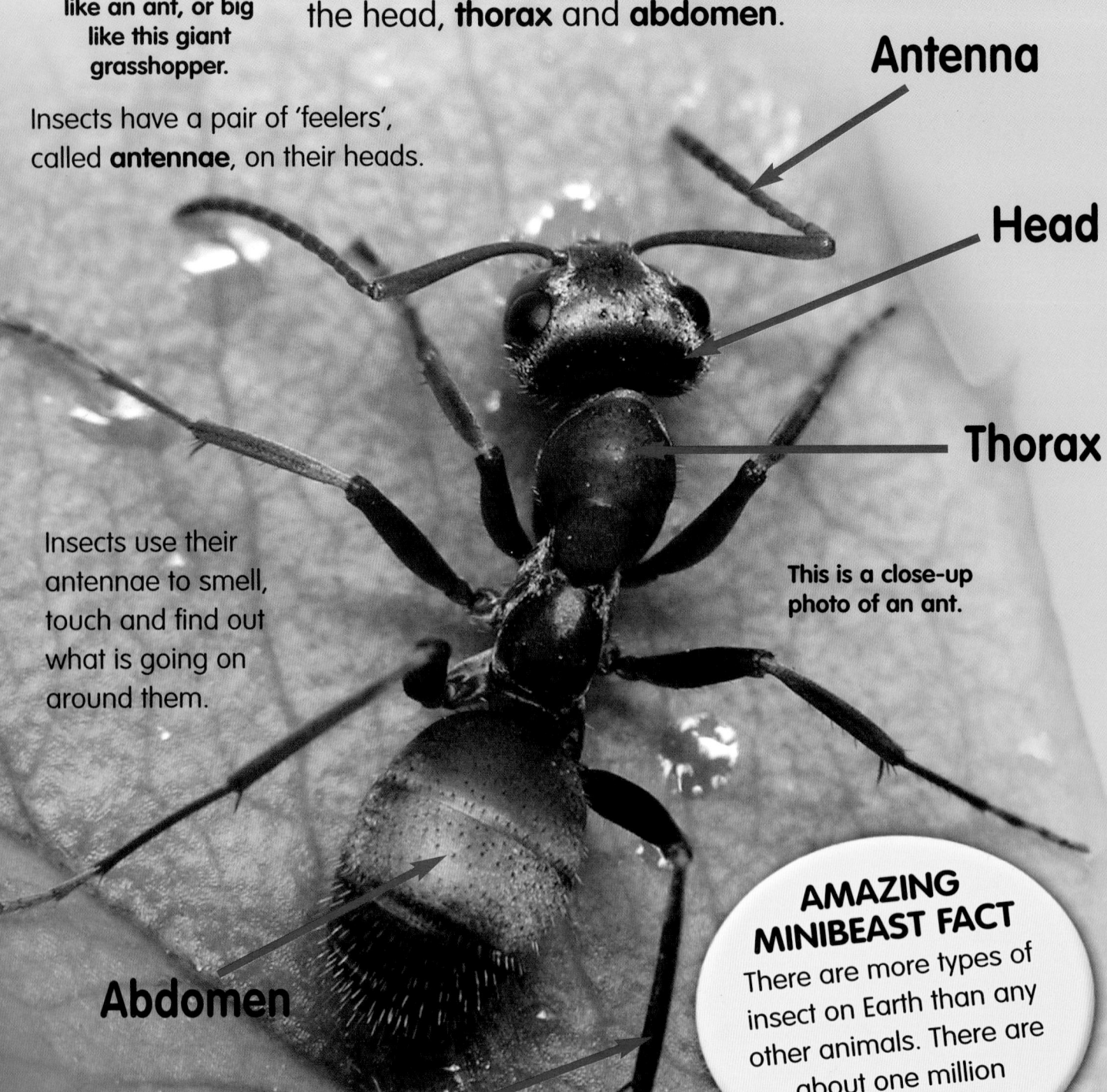

Insects can be tiny like an ant, or big like this giant grasshopper.

Insects have a pair of 'feelers', called **antennae**, on their heads.

Insects use their antennae to smell, touch and find out what is going on around them.

This is a close-up photo of an ant.

Antenna

Head

Thorax

Abdomen

Leg

AMAZING MINIBEAST FACT
There are more types of insect on Earth than any other animals. There are about one million different insects!

4

A dragonfly

Many insects, such as dragonflies, have two pairs of wings. Others have one pair of wings and some insects have no wings.

A fly has one pair of wings.

A flea has no wings.

This fly's eye is made of hundreds of tiny hexagon shapes.

Eye

Insects have 'compound' eyes. Their eyes are made of many small light-gathering sections.

Insect life

Some insects eat only plants. Others hunt and eat other insects. Wasps, bees and butterflies are attracted to brightly coloured flowers where they drink a sweet juice called **nectar**.

Butterflies have a tongue, like a straw, for sipping nectar.

Many insects eat dead wood from rotting trees. The young, or **larvae**, of stag beetles eat rotting wood.

Adult stag beetle

Some insects, such as ants live in big **colonies**. Others, such as adult stag beetles, live alone. Adult males and females get together to **mate**.

AMAZING MINIBEAST FACT
Some beetles use flashes of light, made by special parts under their bodies, to attract a mate.

The female aphid in this photo is giving birth.

A firefly

Female moths produce special smells to attract mates. After mating, the female moth lays lots of eggs. She then leaves the eggs to hatch on their own.

A ruby tiger moth lays eggs on a leaf.

Female aphid

Some insects, such as aphids, can give birth to live young.

What is a spider?

Spiders belong to an animal group called arachnids. All spiders have four pairs of legs and a body in two parts. Spiders are **predators**. They hunt and eat other animals for food.

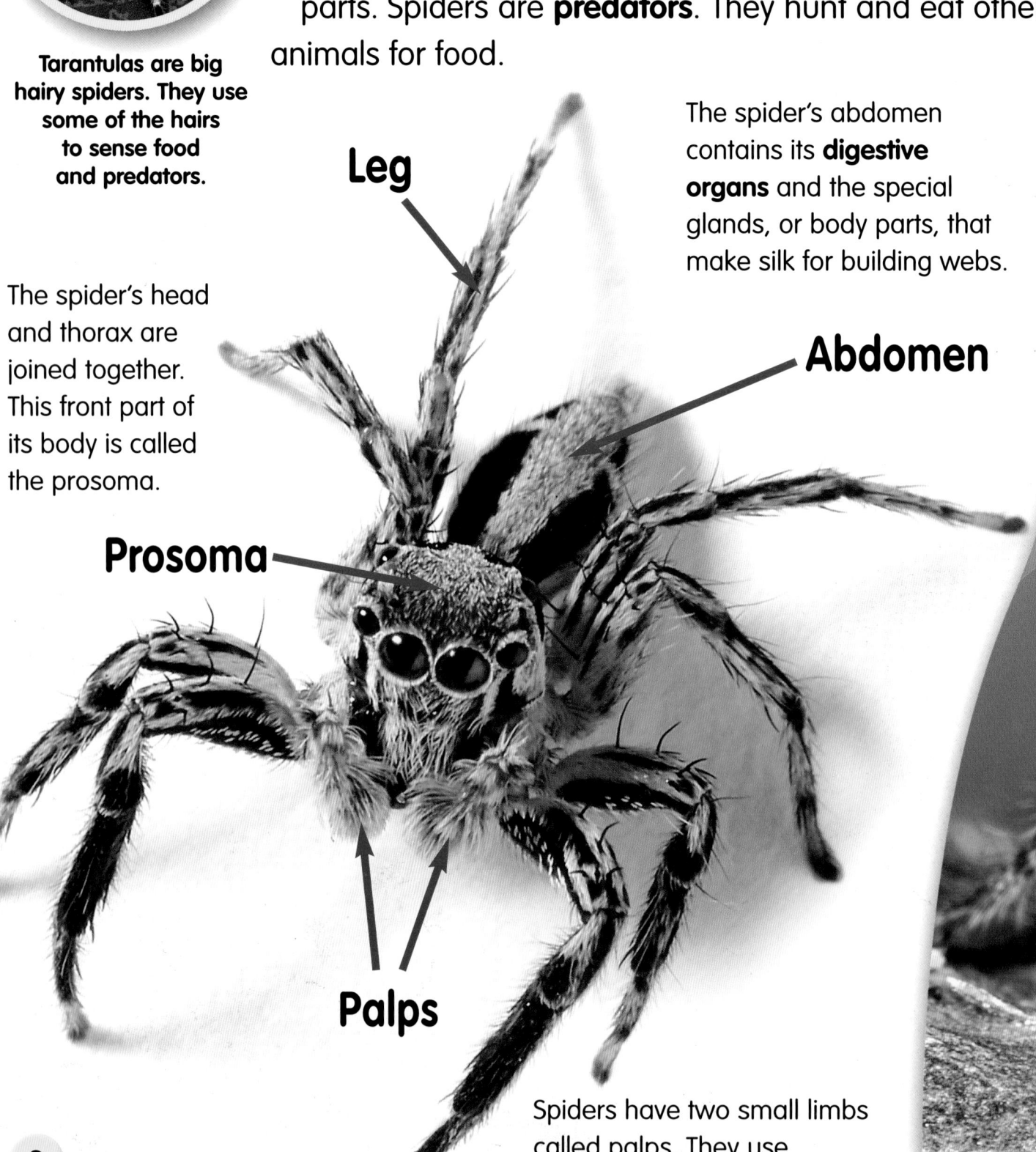

Tarantulas are big hairy spiders. They use some of the hairs to sense food and predators.

The spider's abdomen contains its **digestive organs** and the special glands, or body parts, that make silk for building webs.

The spider's head and thorax are joined together. This front part of its body is called the prosoma.

Leg

Abdomen

Prosoma

Palps

Spiders have two small limbs called palps. They use them for feeling things.

8

Some spiders build webs. They make them out of silk threads. The threads come out of a part of the spider's body called a spinneret.

Web

Orb web spider

Eyes

AMAZING MINIBEAST FACT
Most spiders have eight eyes. All spiders have **fangs** for injecting poison into their **prey**.

This jumping spider has caught a fly and is holding it using its fangs.

Spider life

There are about 35,000 different types of spiders. Webs are a good sign that spiders are around. Webs made by orb spiders can be found on plants, on fences and inside buildings.

For its thickness, spider silk is very strong!

Some spiders sit in the middle of the web ready for prey to arrive.

Other spiders hide away and when their web begins to shake, they know an insect has become trapped in it.

The spider wraps its prey in silk.

AMAZING MINIBEAST FACT
Spider silk is liquid (runny) until it comes out of the spinneret.

This is a tree trunk trapdoor spider.

Trapdoor spiders make underground **burrows** with a door above. When the spider feels something moving close to the door, it jumps out and pulls its prey down into the hole.

Burrow

Trapdoor

Eggs

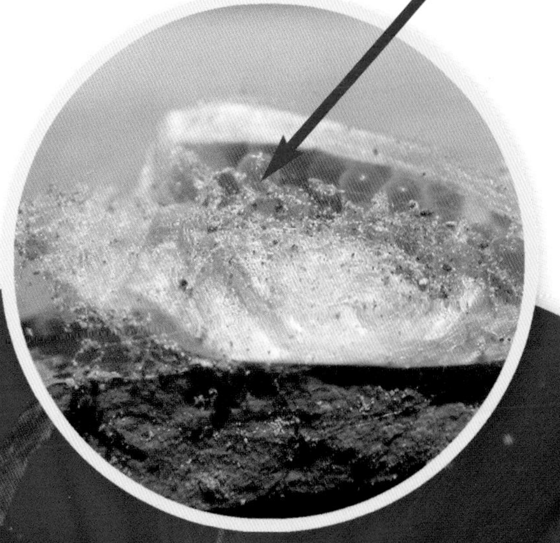

Adult spiders live on their own. Males and females only get together to mate. After mating, the female spider lays lots of eggs and covers them with silk.

Many female spiders leave their eggs. The baby spiders hatch and have to take care of themselves.

This nursery web spider carries her eggs with her in a silk egg sac.

Egg sac

Minibeast habitats

A habitat is the place where a plant or an animal lives. Insects live in habitats from hot **deserts** to cold mountains. Spiders live in lots of habitats, too, but not in very cold places, such as the Arctic or Antarctica.

There can be 2,000 different insects living in a garden.

The ocean is a habitat, but no insects or spiders live in the ocean.

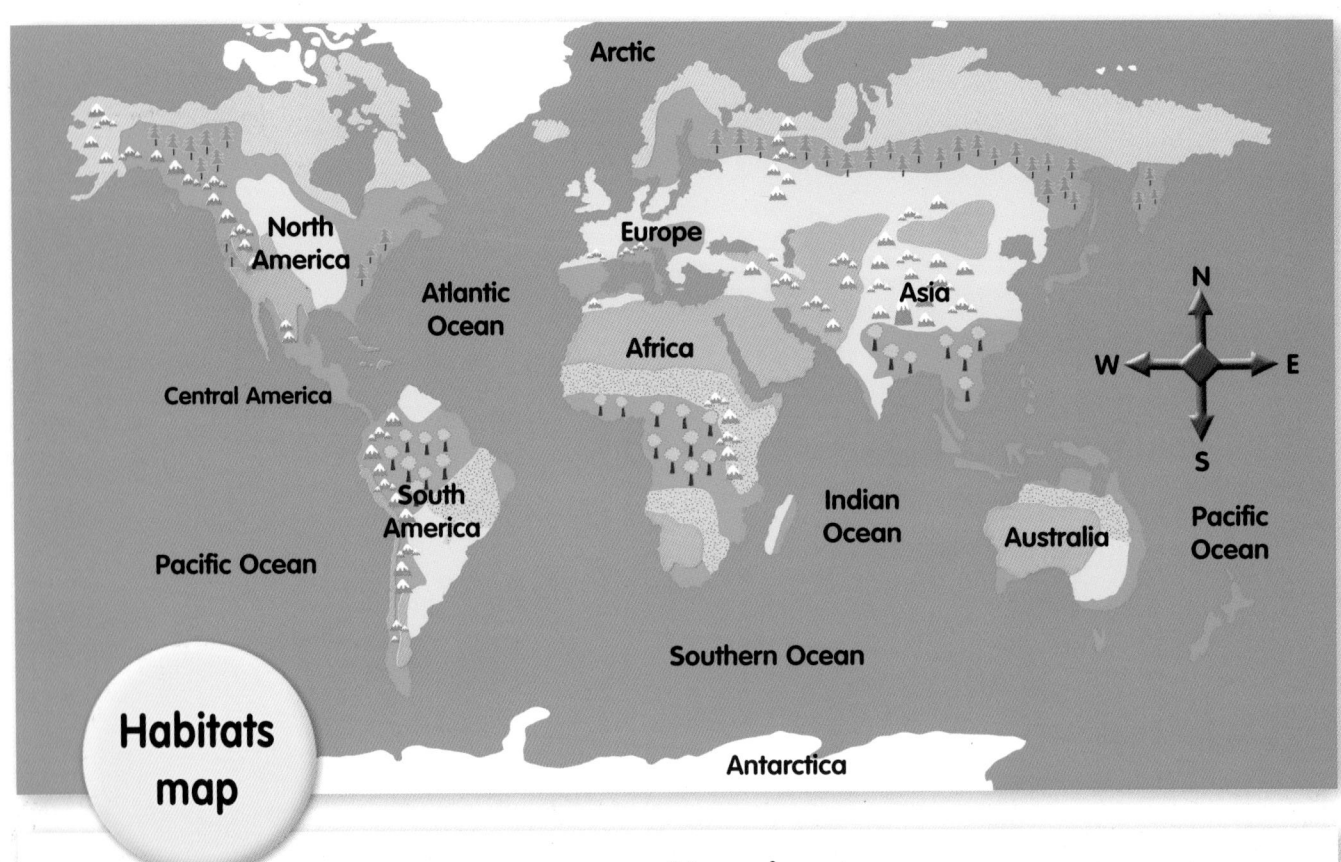

Habitats map

Map key

This map key shows you what the colours and pictures on the map mean.

Temperate grasslands – areas that are dry in summer

Tropical grasslands – hot, dry areas with few trees

Tundra – cold, windy places

Cool, rainy forests

Arctic/Antarctica – frozen, snowy ground and icy seas

Cold forests

Warm, wet rainforest

Deserts – dry land with little rain

Many insects, such as dragonflies, live in or near **freshwater** pools, rivers and lakes.

Dragonflies lay their eggs in ponds.

Leaf-cutter ants grow a **fungus** on the leaves they collect. The ants eat the fungus.

One of the reasons there are so many insects and spiders is because they are small animals and do not need much habitat to live in.

AMAZING MINIBEAST FACT
Rainforests have more insects than any other habitat in the world.

Leaf-cutter ants live in South American rainforests.

Hundreds of different types of insect can live on one oak tree.

What is a life cycle?

A life cycle is all the different **stages** and changes that a plant or animal goes through in its life. The diagrams on these pages show an example of an insect life cycle and a spider life cycle.

Sometimes a female spider thinks a male is prey in her web and eats him!

1

A male and female ladybird meet and mate.

LADYBIRD LIFE CYCLE
Many insects have a life cycle with these stages.

2

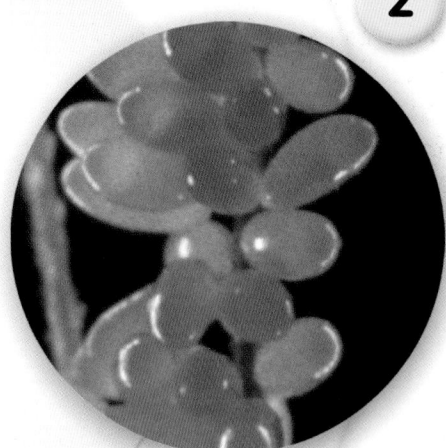

The female ladybird lays lots of eggs. She doesn't look after the eggs or her babies.

4

Inside the case the larva turns into an adult ladybird. This ladybird has just climbed out of its pupal case.

3

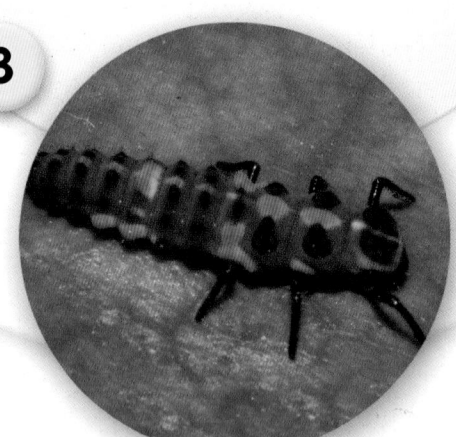

A larva hatches from each egg. The larva eats lots of aphids. Then the larva makes a case around its body and becomes a pupa.

1

An adult male and female spider meet and mate.

SPIDER LIFE CYCLE
Many spiders have a life cycle with these stages.

4

2

The spiderlings moult – their old skin falls off and there's a new, bigger skin underneath. They moult four or five times before they are fully grown.

3

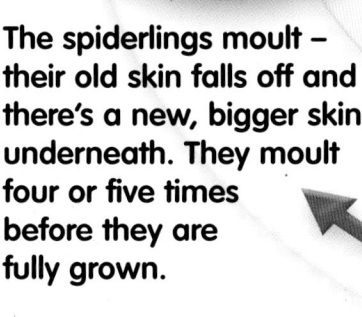

The female lays her eggs in a silk egg sac. Some spiders guard their eggs, others leave them.

The spiderlings hatch. Some spiderlings make a tangled web. The spiderlings grow bigger. Their hard outer skin gets too small.

Praying mantid

Amazing minibeast life cycles

Jumping spider

In this book we are going to find out about some amazing life cycles – from praying mantids to jumping spiders.

There can be
50 billion desert
locusts in one swarm.

Locust

A swarm of locusts can eat a huge field of wheat in minutes! In a single day a swarm of desert locusts can eat four times as much food as all the humans living in London.

After mating, a female locust pushes her body deep into the soil. She lays 100 eggs one after the other. Female insects lay their eggs through a tube called an ovipositor.

Ovipositor

AMAZING MINIBEAST FACT
Female locusts make a sort of foam that protects their eggs.

Foam

Eggs

16

Tiny locust larvae called nymphs or hoppers hatch from the eggs.

Hopper

Large groups of hoppers are called bands. As they march along, they eat all the plants in their path.

As the hoppers grow their skin becomes too tight. It splits and drops off. This is called moulting. There is a new skin underneath.

Adult locust

After they have moulted five times, the young hoppers become adults with wings.

Wing

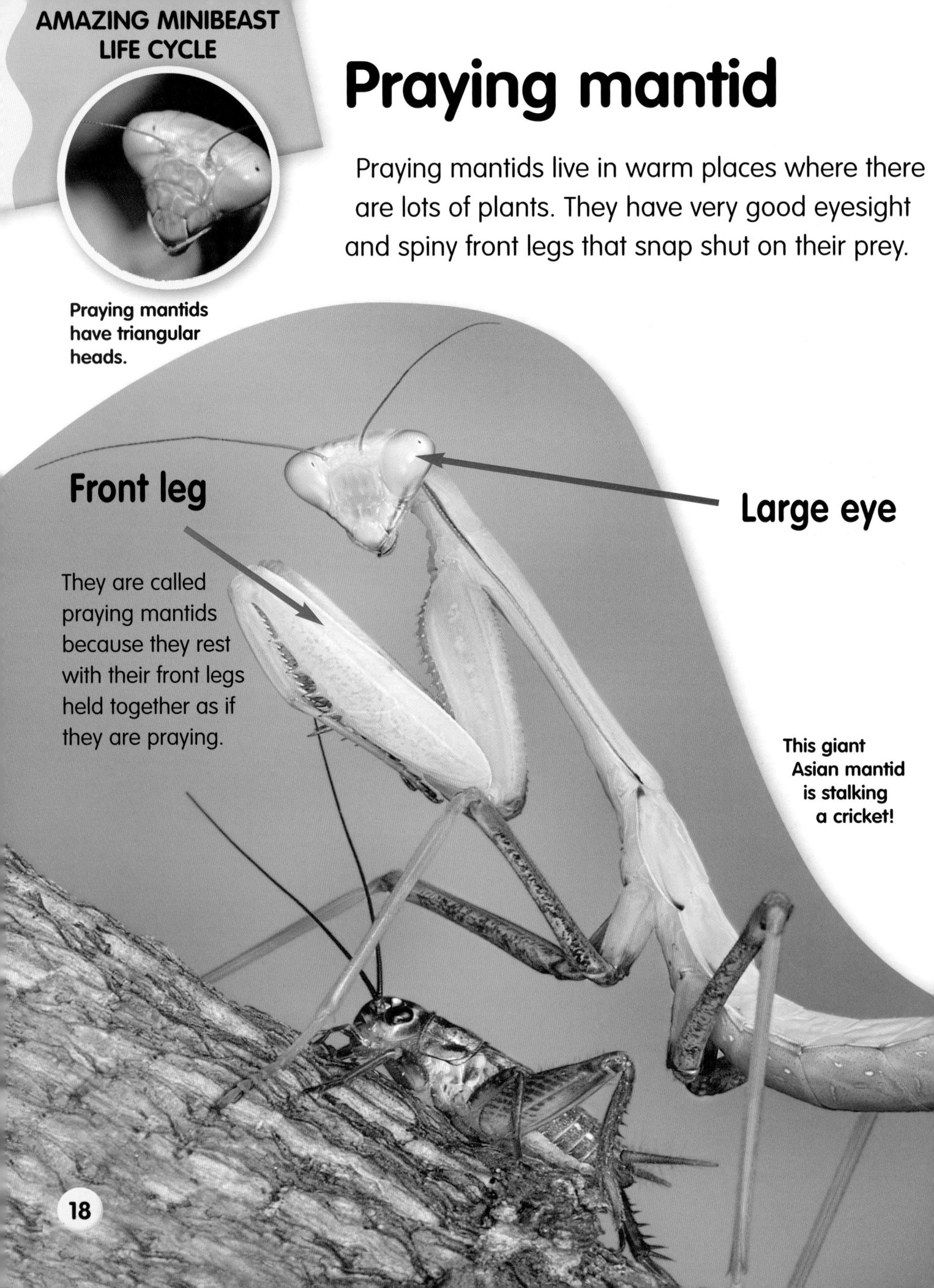

Praying mantids have triangular heads.

Praying mantid

Praying mantids live in warm places where there are lots of plants. They have very good eyesight and spiny front legs that snap shut on their prey.

Front leg

They are called praying mantids because they rest with their front legs held together as if they are praying.

Large eye

This giant Asian mantid is stalking a cricket!

18

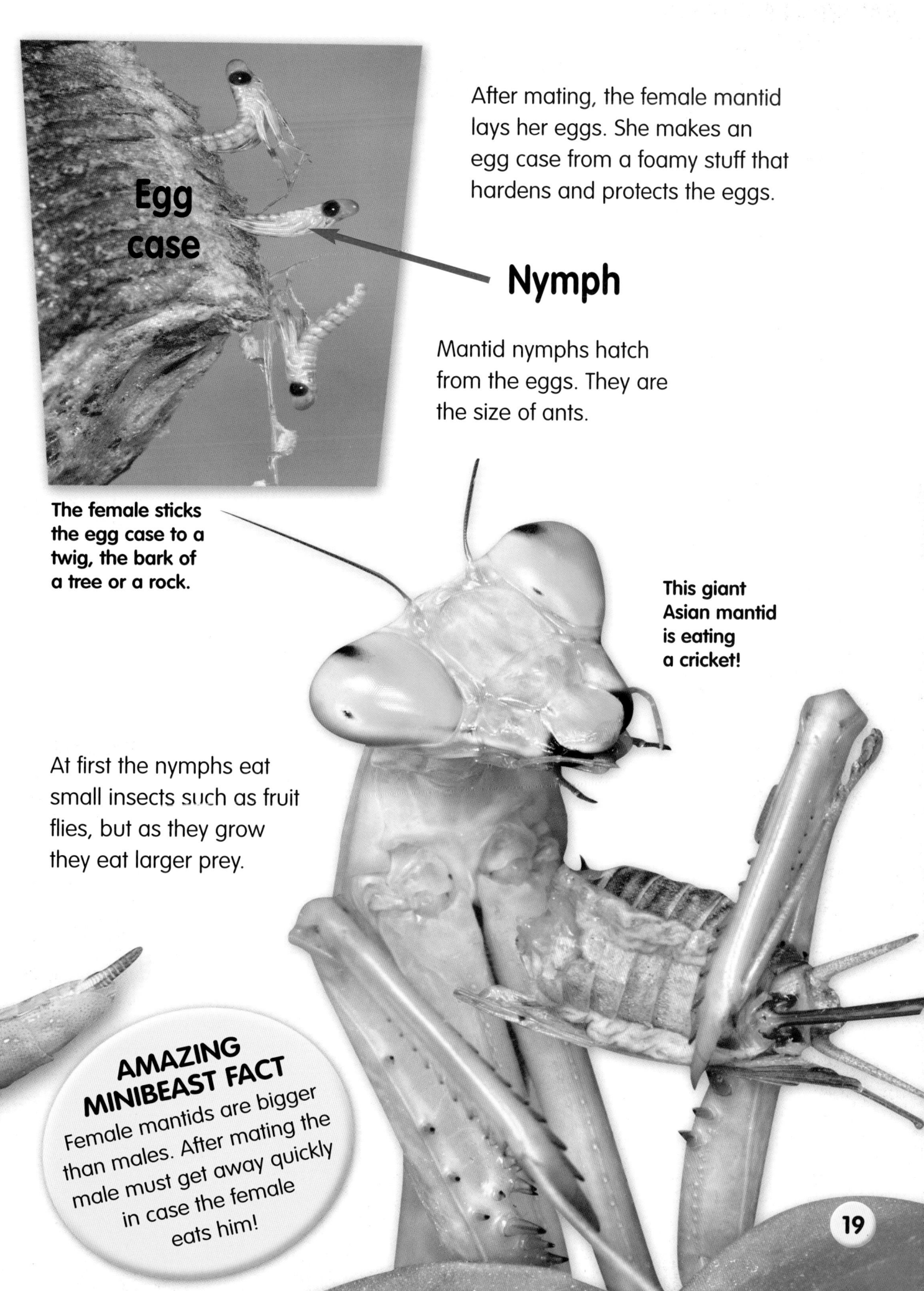

Egg case

After mating, the female mantid lays her eggs. She makes an egg case from a foamy stuff that hardens and protects the eggs.

Nymph

Mantid nymphs hatch from the eggs. They are the size of ants.

The female sticks the egg case to a twig, the bark of a tree or a rock.

This giant Asian mantid is eating a cricket!

At first the nymphs eat small insects such as fruit flies, but as they grow they eat larger prey.

AMAZING MINIBEAST FACT
Female mantids are bigger than males. After mating the male must get away quickly in case the female eats him!

Only male rhino beetles have a horn.

Rhinoceros beetle

The rhinoceros, or rhino, beetle lives in rainforests. This beetle gets its name from its horn that looks like a rhino's horn!

This rhino beetle is five centimetres long.

AMAZING MINIBEAST FACT
Adult rhino beetles feed on nectar, rotting fruit and **sap** from trees and plants.

Male rhino beetles sometimes use their horns to fight over **territory** with other males. If the male has a good territory with plenty of food, he will be able to attract a female.

After mating, the female rhino beetle lays her eggs. The eggs hatch into larvae. After two to three years, each larva becomes a **pupa**.

A rhino beetle larva eats rotting wood and dead leaves.

Pupa

Inside its pupal case, the larva turns into an adult rhino beetle. This takes about four to six weeks.

All butterflies have two pairs of wings.

Birdwing butterfly

Butterflies live in lots of different habitats – from rainforests to city gardens. There are about 17,000 different types of butterflies. The Queen Alexandra birdwing is the biggest butterfly in the world.

The male and female Queen Alexandra birdwing butterflies look different to each other. The female is bigger than the male.

Male

28 cm

This butterfly's wingspan is bigger than the wingspan of some birds!

Female

22

All butterflies have the same kind of life cycle.

A male and female butterfly meet and mate. The female lays lots of eggs. Larvae, called caterpillars, hatch from the eggs. They eat and eat.

This is a monarch butterfly caterpillar.

The caterpillar gets too big for its skin. The old skin moults and there's a new skin underneath. The caterpillar moults several times.

This photo shows the caterpillar making its case.

Then the caterpillar makes a case around its body and becomes a pupa.

Inside the pupal case, the caterpillar becomes a butterfly!

AMAZING MINIBEAST FACT
The Queen Alexandra birdwing butterfly only lives in Papua New Guinea in South East Asia.

This monarch butterfly is crawling out of its case.

23

A spider-hunting wasp sting can be very painful to humans.

Spider-hunting wasp

There are about 4,000 different types of spider-hunting wasps in the world. The female wasp will fly above the ground or run about tapping the ground with her antennae hunting for spiders.

When the female wasp catches a spider, she fights with the spider and stings it so it is paralysed. This means it cannot move, but it is still alive.

Antenna

Wings

Wolf spider

Burrow

The wasp then drags the spider to a burrow she has dug and pulls the spider underground.

The paralysed spider cannot escape!

AMAZING MINIBEAST FACT
Some types of spider-hunting wasp are seven centimetres long! Most types are under 25 millimetres long.

The female lays a single egg on the spider and then seals the burrow. When the egg hatches, the young wasp larva eats the spider alive!

The wasp larva spins a silk case called a cocoon. Inside the cocoon it becomes an adult wasp. The new adult wasp crawls to the surface and escapes from the burrow.

Jumping spider

**Most jumping spiders
have hairy bodies.**

Jumping spiders live in forests, in woodland, in gardens and many other habitats around the world. There are about 5,000 different types of jumping spider.

Jumping spiders have eight eyes – two of the eyes are very big like car headlights. The spider's big eyes help it to spot its insect prey, and judge the distance of its jump.

Jumping spiders jump to catch prey, and to escape from predators, such as birds.

The jumping spider in this photo is pouncing on a hover fly. The spider attaches a safety line of silk in case it misses its landing spot.

Silk safety line

Hover fly

AMAZING MINIBEAST FACT
The jumping spider can leap up to 25 times the length of its own body!

This female has hidden her egg sac in a dead leaf.

After mating the female jumping spider lays lots of eggs in one go. She wraps them in an egg sac made of silk thread.

The female guards her eggs until the spiderlings hatch.

Large water spiders eat
baby fish and tadpoles.

Water spider

The water spider lives underwater in ponds or
slow flowing rivers. It lives in a diving bell, like a
bubble, made out of silk which it fills with air.

The spider sits inside the
diving bell. When prey,
such as an insect,
passes, the spider
rushes out,
grabs the prey
and takes it
back to the
bell to eat.

The spider sits with
just its front legs
dangling in the water.
Its head is in the bell
so it can breathe.

The male and female water spider mate inside the female's diving bell.

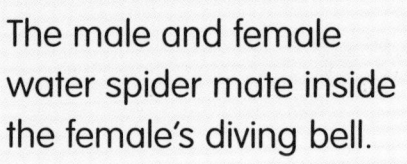

Female

Male

The female lays up to 100 eggs in an egg sac, which she places in the upper part of the diving bell.

When the eggs hatch, the spiderlings stay inside until they moult. Then they leave to make diving bell homes of their own.

That's amazing!

Most insects and spiders do not care for their eggs or young, but there are some amazing minibeast parents. These good mums feed their babies and protect them from being eaten by predators.

The wolf spider carries her spiderlings on her back.

A female earwig looks after her eggs inside an underground burrow. She licks them every day to stop fungus from growing on them.

Insects such as bees and wasps live in large groups and make a nest in which to look after their young.

Earwig

Eggs

Cell →

↖ **Egg**

Paper wasp

Paper wasps make a nest of papery chewed up wood.

A female queen bee or wasp lays all the eggs. An egg is laid in each cell of the nest. Larvae hatch from the eggs.

The other females in the group, called workers, help to look after the nest and feed the larvae.

AMAZING MINIBEAST FACT
Female paper wasps feed their larvae on chewed up insects.

This paper wasp larva has grown into an adult. It is climbing out of its cell.

31

Glossary

abdomen – The part of an animal's body that contains the digestive organs.

antennae – A pair of 'feelers' used by an insect to touch and smell its environment.

burrows – Tunnels and holes under the ground where some animals live.

colonies – Large groups.

deserts – Very dry places, that are often sandy or rocky. Deserts can be very hot in the day. Some deserts get cold at night.

digestive organs – The body parts that digest food, such as the stomach.

fangs – Very sharp teeth.

freshwater – Rainwater, and the water in ponds and some rivers. It is not salty.

fungus – A very simple living thing that grows and spreads. Another word we use for some types of fungus is mould.

larvae – The young of some insects.

mate – When a male and female animal meet and have babies.

nectar – A sweet liquid inside flowers.

predators – Animals which hunt and kill other animals for food.

prey – Animals which are hunted by other animals as food.

pupa – The stage in the life cycle of some insects between a larva and an adult.

sap – A liquid in trees and plants.

stages – Different times of an animal's life when the animal changes.

territory – An area or place where an animal feeds, mates and has its young.

thorax – The middle part of an insect's body. The legs and wings are attached to the thorax.

Index